ARTIST
TRANSCRIPTIONS
PIANO

The Ahmad Jamal Collection

MW00668619

TRANSCRIPTIONS
"Ahmad's Blues"-by Alex Smith
"But Not for Me"-by Alex Smith
"The Canteen"-by Bruce Cameron Munson & Todd Lowry
"For My Daughter"-by Anthony M. Kelley
"My Flower"-by Bruce Cameron Munson & Todd Lowry
"New Rhumba"-by Bruce Cameron Munson & Todd Lowry
"Night Mist Blues"-by Bruce Cameron Munson & David Berger
"Poinciana"-by Alex Smith
"Sumayah"-by Bruce Cameron Munson
"The Surrey with the Fringe on Top"-by Alex Smith

Cover Photo: Mark Norberg

ISBN 0-7935-4854-3

HAL•LEONARD®
CORPORATION
7777 W. BLUEMOUND RD. P.O. BOX 13819 MILWAUKEE, WI 53213

Visit Hal Leonard Online at
www.halleonard.com

Contents

Ahmad Jamal

In 1949, he created his first jazz group called The Three Strings. His first records appeared in 1950 for the Okeh label, a subsidiary of Columbia Records, and they created a small stir in the jazz community. Jamal played acclaimed appearances at the Blue Note in Chicago and the Embers in New York. In 1955, he was signed to the Argo label and began recording in earnest. One of those tunes recorded was "New Rhumba," later to be recorded by Miles Davis and the Gil Evans Orchestra.

Jamal's album *But Not for Me*, recorded at the Pershing Hotel in Chicago, became a smash hit in 1958, and established the Jamal trio as not only an important jazz attraction, but as a 'crossover' act, since the album appealed to the non-jazz listener as well as fans of the music. The album reached number three in the Billboard album charts, remaining there for one hundred and seven weeks. In particular, the recording of "Poinciana" became a radio and jukebox hit. Many best-selling albums followed for the Argo label.

Jamal's success continued in the '60s, with appearances around the world with his trio and several bookings with symphony orchestra accompaniment. In 1970, Jamal's recording of the "Theme from M*A*S*H*" became a hit.

Jamal was awarded an American Jazz Master Fellowship by the National Endowment of the Arts in 1994, and was made a Duke Ellington Fellow of Yale University. In 1995, the motion picture *The Bridges of Madison County* featured his recordings of "Poinciana" and "Music, Music, Music." In 1996, he won the Django D'Or Award for his album *The Essence - Part 1*.

Ahmad Jamal continues to perform worldwide with his trio and as a soloist.

NEW RHUMBA

Written by AHMAD JAMAL

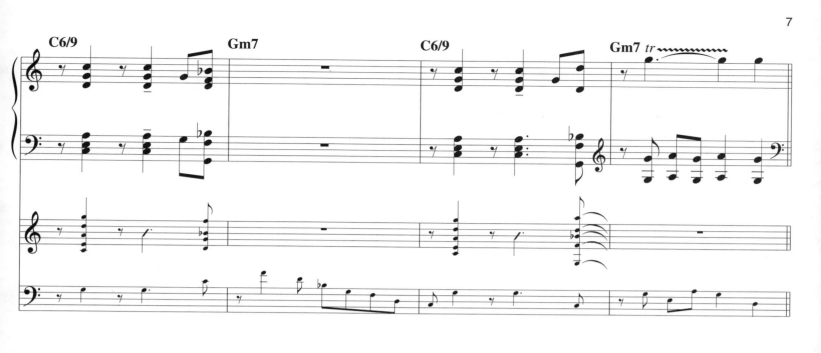

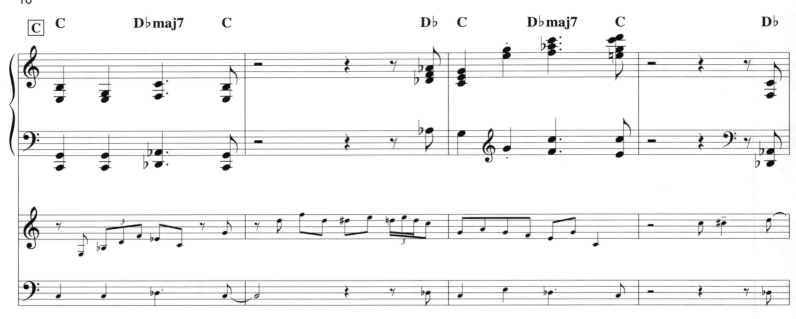

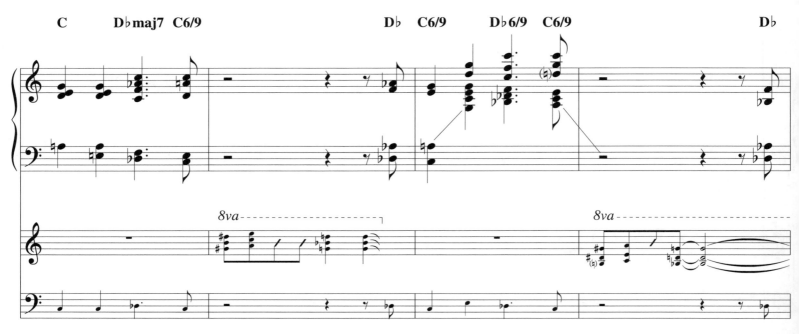

POINCIANA
(Song of the Tree)

Words by BUDDY BERNIER
Music by NAT SIMON

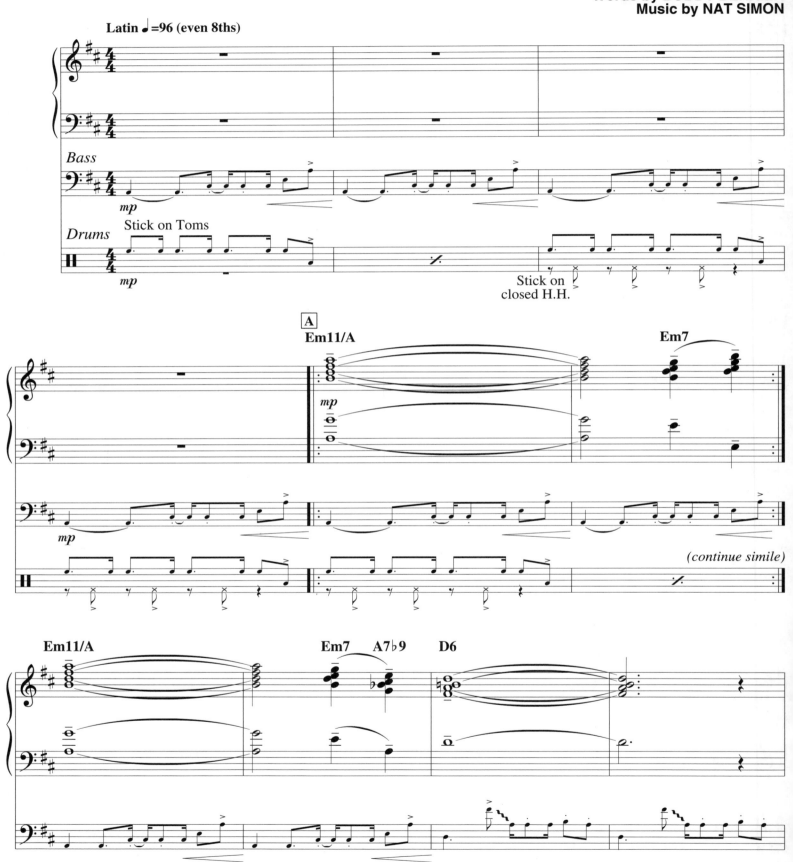

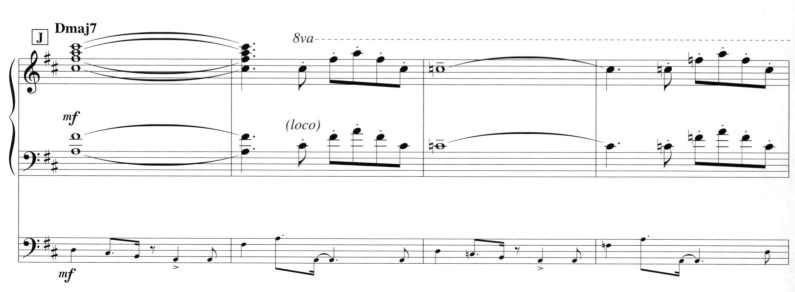

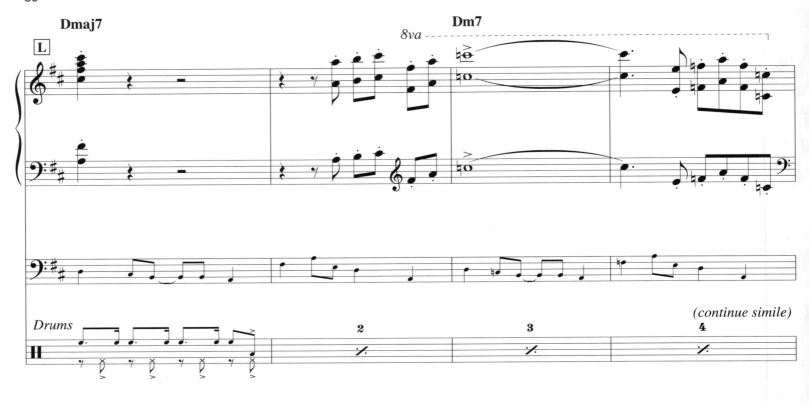

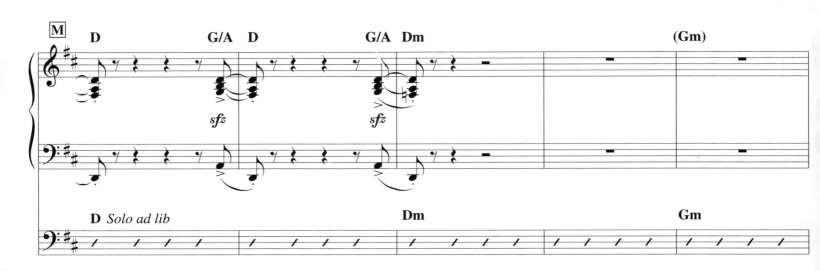

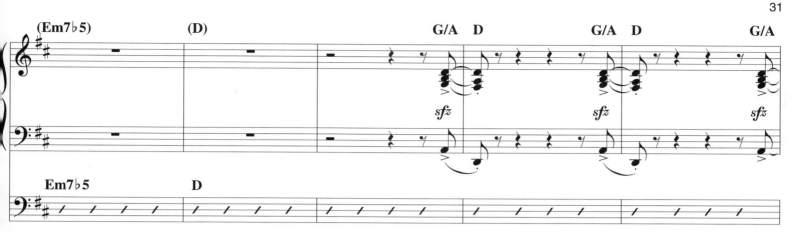

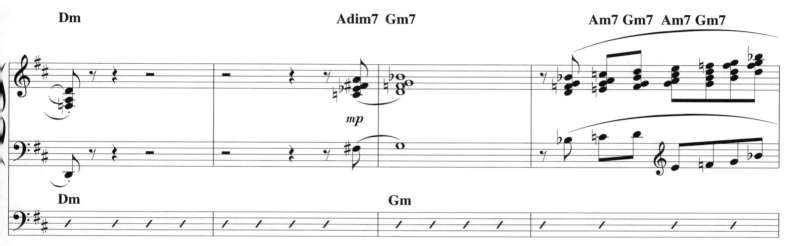

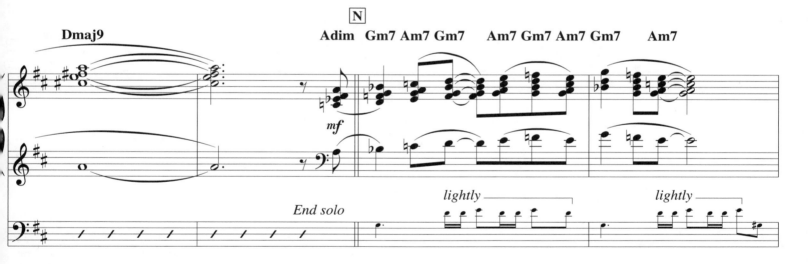

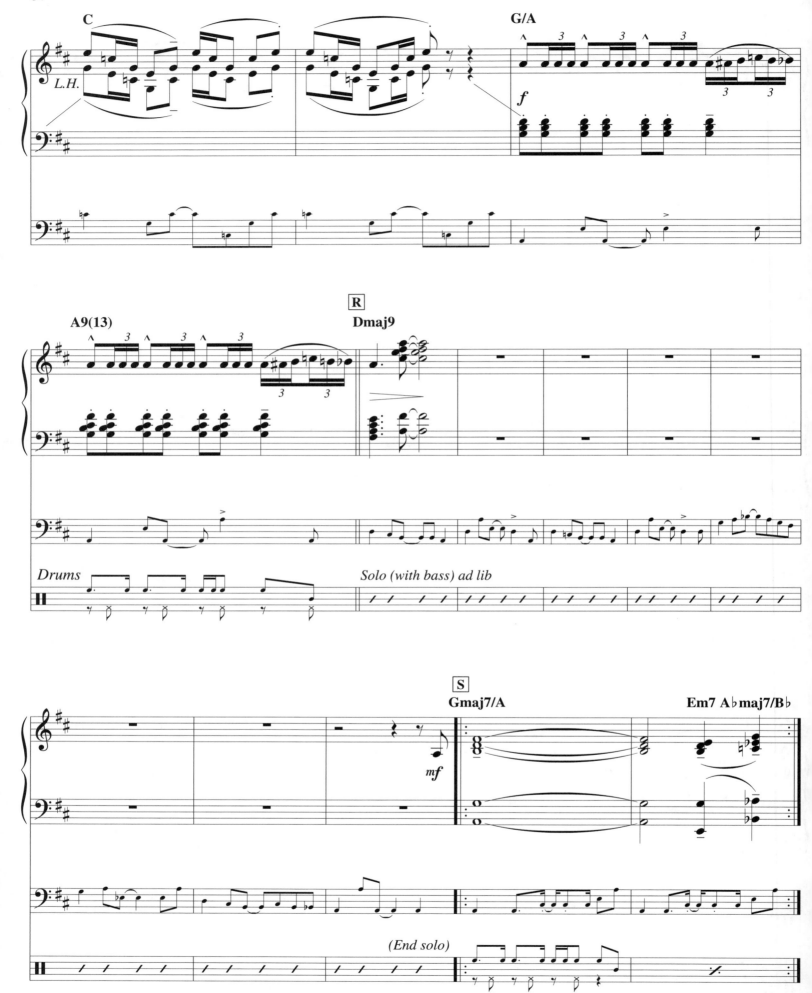

BUT NOT FOR ME

**Music and Lyrics by George Gershwin
and Ira Gershwin**

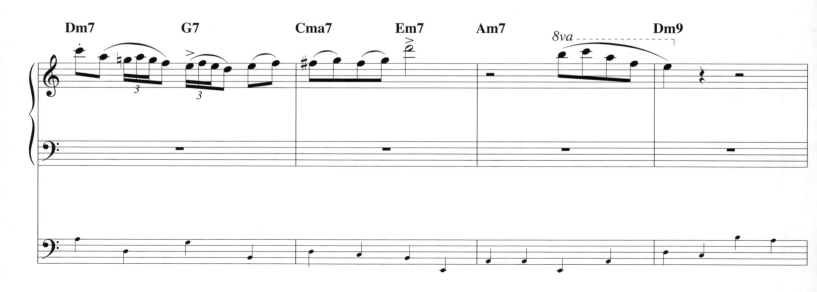

THE SURREY WITH THE FRINGE ON TOP

from OKLAHOMA!

Lyrics by OSCAR HAMMERSTIEN II
Music by RICHARD RODGERS

46

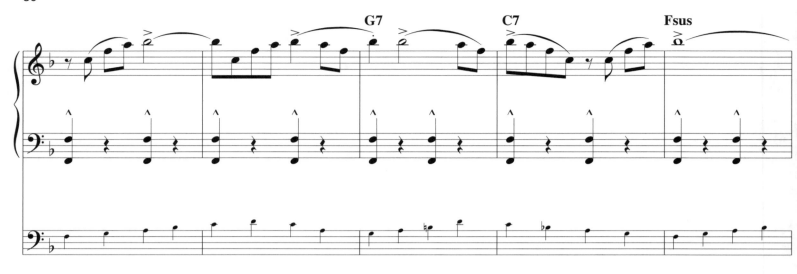

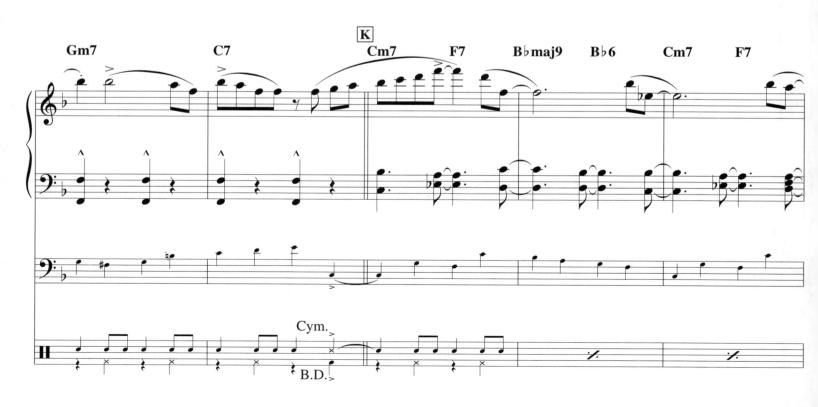

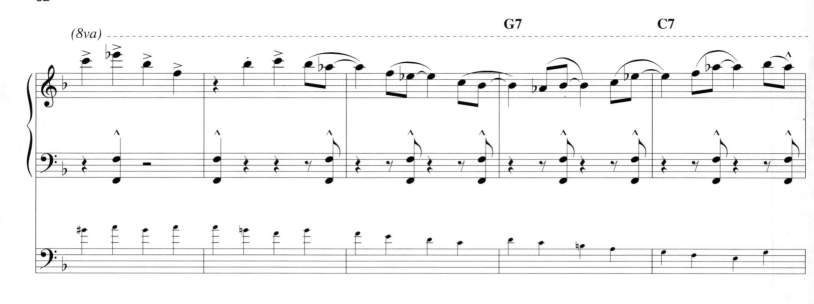

AHMAD'S BLUES

Written by AHMAD JAMAL

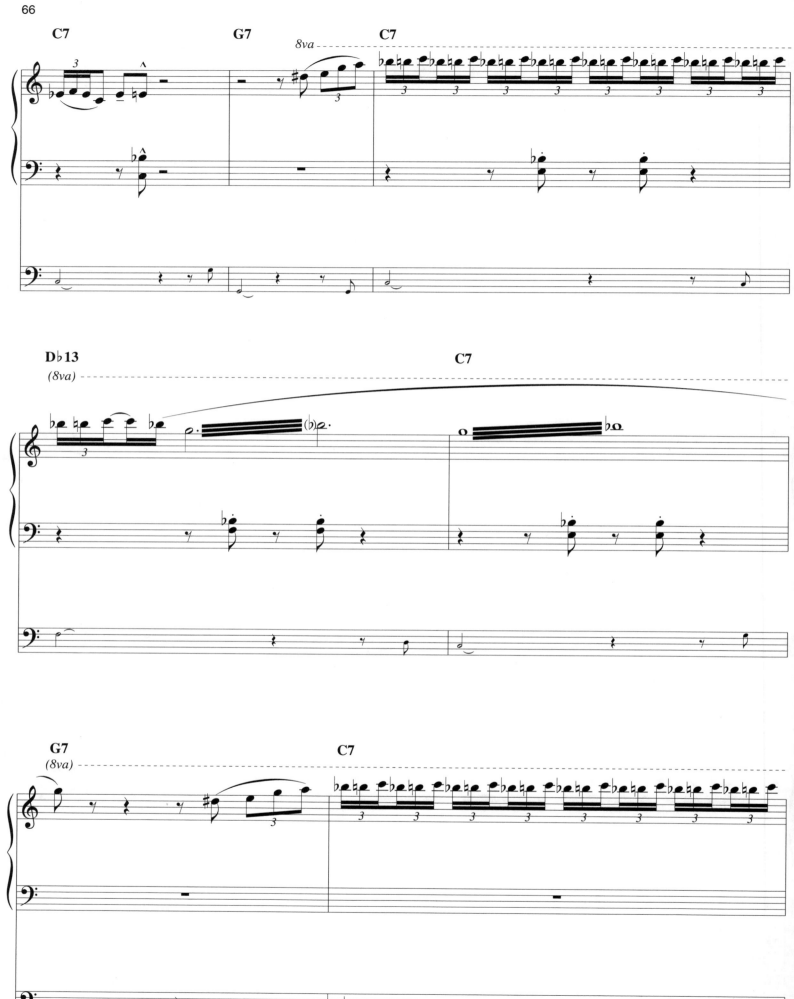

NIGHT MIST BLUES

Written by AHMAD JAMAL

Drums *sim.*

Drums *sim.*

SUMAYAH

Written by AHMAD JAMAL

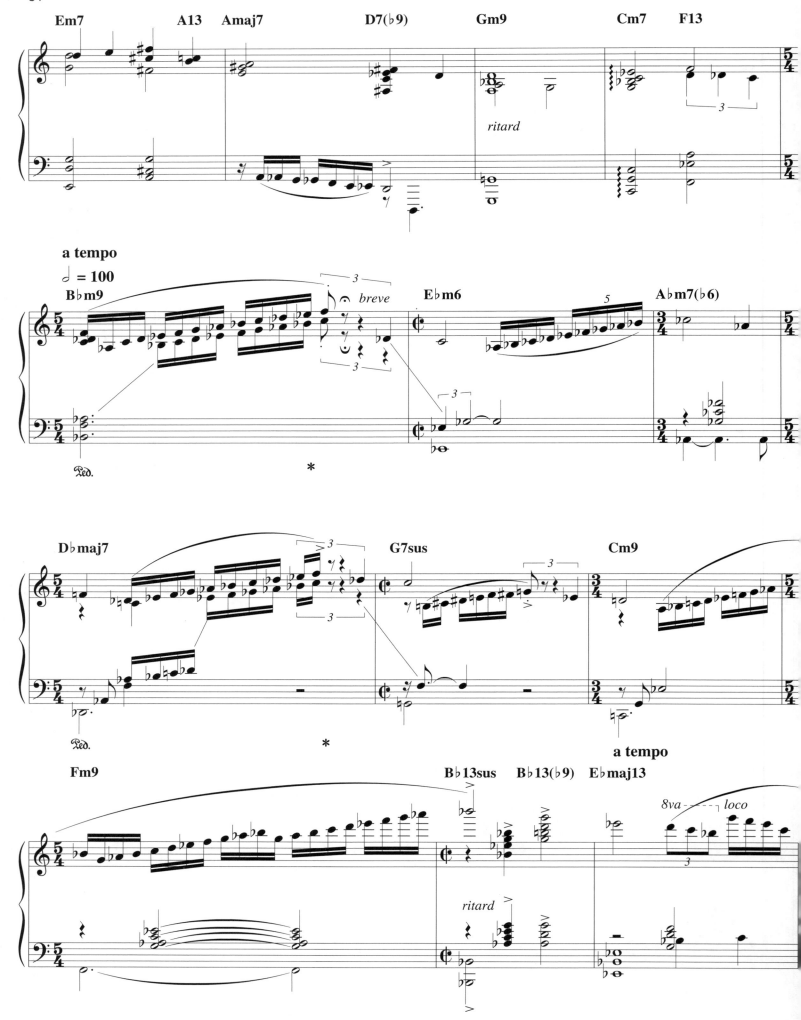

FOR MY DAUGHTER

Written by AHMAD JAMAL

THE CANTEEN

Written by AHMAD JAMAL

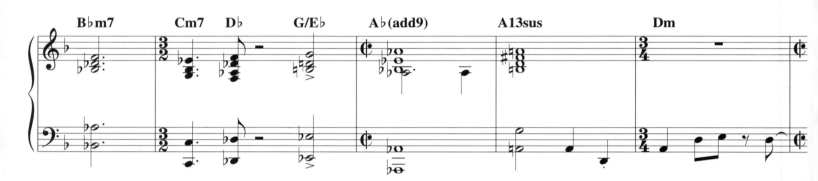

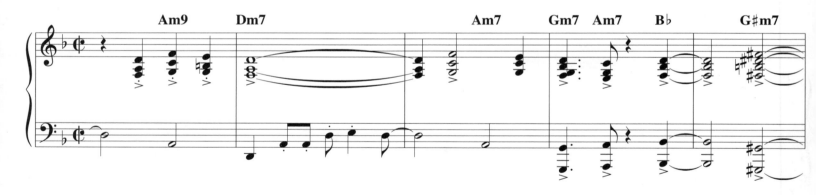

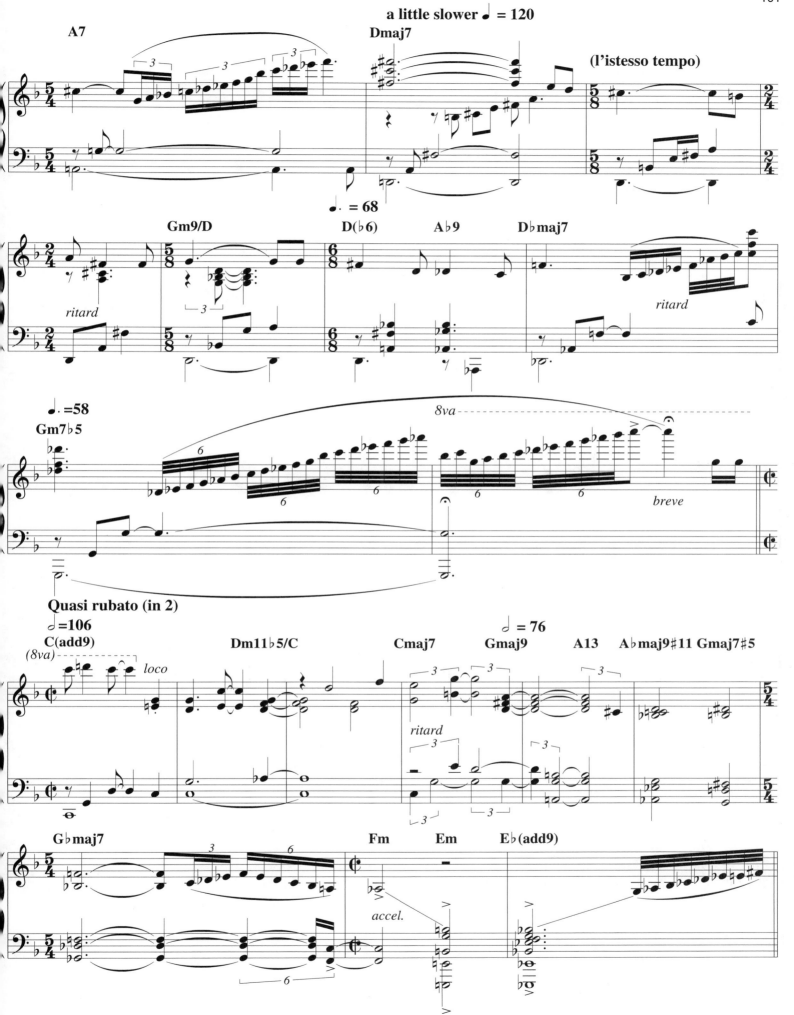

MY FLOWER

Written by AHMAD JAMAL

ARTIST TRANSCRIPTIONS

Artist Transcriptions are authentic, note-for-note transcriptions of the hottest artists in jazz, pop, and rock today. These outstanding, accurate arrangements are in an easy-to-read format which includes all essential lines. Artist Transcriptions can be used to perform, sequence or reference.

Guitar & Bass

The Guitar Book Of Pierre Bensusan
00699072 ....$19.95

Ron Carter – Acoustic Bass
00672331 ....$16.95

Charley Christian – The Art Of Jazz Guitar
00026704 ....$6.95

Stanley Clarke Collection
00672307 ....$19.95

Larry Coryell – Jazz Guitar Solos
00699140 ....$9.95

Al Di Meola – Cielo E Terra
00604041 ....$14.95

Al Di Meola – Friday Night In San Francisco
00660115 ....$14.95

Al Di Meola – Music, Words, Pictures
00604043 ....$14.95

Kevin Eubanks Guitar Collection
00672319 ....$19.95

The Jazz Style Of Tal Farlow
00673245 ....$19.95

Bela Fleck and the Flecktones
00672359 Melody/Lyrics/Chords $14.95

David Friesen – Departure
00673221 ....$14.95

David Friesen – Years Through Time
00673253 ....$14.95

Frank Gambale
00673223 ....$19.95

Best Of Frank Gambale
00672336 ....$19.95

Jim Hall – Jazz Guitar Environments
00699388 Book/Cassette...........................$17.95
00699389 Book/CD....................................$19.95

Jim Hall – Exploring Jazz Guitar
00699306 ....$16.95

Scott Henderson Guitar Book
00699330 ....$19.95

**Allan Holdsworth –
Reaching For The Uncommon Chord**
00604049 ....$14.95

Leo Kottke – Eight Songs
00699215 ....$14.95

Wes Montgomery – Guitar Transcriptions
00675536 ....$14.95

John Patitucci
00673216 ....$14.95

Django Reinhardt Anthology
00027083 ....$14.95

The Genius of Django Reinhardt
00026711 ....$10.95

Django Reinhardt – A Treasury of Songs
00026715 ....$12.95

John Renbourn – The Nine Maidens, The Hermit, Stefan and John
00699071 ....$12.95

Prices and availability subject to change without notice. Some products may not be available outside the U.S.A.

Great Rockabilly Guitar Solos
00692820 ....$14.95

John Scofield – Guitar Transcriptions
00603390 ....$16.95

Segovia, Andres – 20 Studies For The Guitar
00006362 Book/Cassette $14.95

Mike Stern Guitar Book
00673224 ....$16.95

Mark Whitfield
00672320 ....$19.95

Jack Wilkins – Windows
00673249 ....$14.95

Gary Willis Collection
00672337 ....$19.95

Flute

James Newton – Improvising Flute
00660108 ....$14.95

Piano & Keyboard

Monty Alexander Collection
00672338 ....$19.95

Kenny Barron Collection
00672318 ....$22.95

Warren Bernhardt Collection
00672364 ....$19.95

Billy Childs Collection
00673242 ....$19.95

Chick Corea – Beneath The Mask
00673225 ....$12.95

Chick Corea – Inside Out
00673209 ....$12.95

Chick Corea – Eye Of The Beholder
00660007 ....$14.95

Chick Corea – Light Years
00674305 ....$14.95

Chick Corea – Elektric Band
00603126 ....$15.95

Chick Corea – Paint The World
00672300 ....$12.95

Benny Green Collection
00672329 ....$19.95

Ahmad Jamal Collection
00672322 ....$19.95

Michel Petrucciani
00673226 ....$17.95

Joe Sample – Ashes To Ashes
00672310 ....$14.95

Horace Silver Collection
00672303 ....$19.95

Art Tatum Collection
00672316 ....$22.95

Billy Taylor Collection
00672357 ....$24.95

McCoy Tyner
00673215 ....$14.95

Saxophone

Julian "Cannonball" Adderly Collection
00673244 ....$16.95

Michael Brecker
00673237 ....$16.95

The Brecker Brothers...And All Their Jazz
00672351 ....$19.95

Benny Carter Plays Standards
00672315 ....$22.95

Benny Carter Collection
00672314 ....$19.95

John Coltrane – Giant Steps
00672349 ....$19.95

John Coltrane Solos
00673233 ....$22.95

Paul Desmond Collection
00672328 ....$19.95

Stan Getz
00699375 ....$14.95

Great Tenor Sax Solos
00673254 ....$18.95

Joe Henderson – Selections from "Lush Life" & "So Near So Far"
00673252 ....$19.95

Best Of Joe Henderson
00672330 ....$22.95

Best Of Kenny G
00673239 ....$19.95

Kenny G – Breathless
00673229 ....$19.95

Joe Lovano Collection
00672326 ....$19.95

The Art Pepper Collection
00672301 ....$19.95

David Sanborn Collection
00675000 ....$14.95

Best Of David Sanborn
00120891 ....$14.95

Wayne Shorter Saxophone Transcriptions
00660120 ....$14.95

Stanley Turrentine Collection
00672334 ....$19.95

Ernie Watts Saxophone Collection
00673256 ....$18.95

Trombone

J.J. Johnson Collection
00672332 ....$19.95

Trumpet

Randy Brecker
00673234 ....$14.95

Freddie Hubbard
00673214 ....$14.95

The Brecker Brothers...And All Their Jazz
00672351 ....$19.95

Tom Harrell Jazz Trumpet
00672382 ....$19.95

FOR MORE INFORMATION, SEE YOUR LOCAL MUSIC DEALER, OR WRITE TO:

HAL•LEONARD®
CORPORATION

7777 W. BLUEMOUND RD. P.O. BOX 13819 MILWAUKEE, WI 53213

1297

Selected Discography

POINCIANA (1951-55)
    (Okeh recordings)   CD- PORTRAIT RJ 44394

CHAMBER MUSIC OF THE NEW JAZZ   ARGO LP 602
    (1955 - New Rhumba)

BUT NOT FOR ME/AHMAD JAMAL AT THE PERSHING
    (1/16,17/58)   ARGO LP 628
    (But Not for Me, Poinciana,   CD - CHESS CHD 9108
    The Surrey with the Fringe on Top)

AHMAD'S BLUES   ARGO LP 2638
    (9/5,6/58 - Ahmad's Blues)   CD - GRP GRD 803

AHMAD JAMAL AT THE BLACKHAWK   ARGO LP 703
    (9/62 - Night Mist Blues)

THE AWAKENING (1970)   IMPULSE AS 9194
                                CD - IMPULSE 5644

JAMAL PLAYS JAMAL (1973)   20TH CENTURY FOX T432

ONE (1988 - Sumayah)   20TH CENTURY FOX T555

LIVE IN CONCERT (1981)   CHIAROSCURO CR 2036

DIGITAL WORKS (1982)   CD - ATLANTIC 80699-2

ROSSITER ROAD (1985)   CD - ATLANTIC 81645-2

LIVE AT MONTREUX JAZZ FESTIVAL   CD - ATLANTIC 81699-2
    (1986)

CRYSTAL (1987 - The Canteen,   CD - ATLANTIC 81793-2
    For My Daughter)

LIVE AT JOE SEGAL: CHICAGO REVISITED   CD - TELARC CD 83327
    (1993)

I REMEMBER DUKE, HOAGY AND STRAYHORN   CD - TELARC CD 83339
    (1994 - My Flower)

THE ESSENCE - PART 1 (1996)   CD - VERVE 529 327 - 2

THE ESSENCE - PART 2 (1997)   CD - VERVE 314 533 477 - 2

Biography

Ahmad Jamal is one of those rare musicians whose art has influenced a widely varied group of jazz artists, from pianists such as Red Garland, Benny Green and Cedar Walton, to Miles Davis, who recorded Ahmad's compositions and other songs in Jamal's repertoire ("Surrey with the Fringe on Top" and "Squeeze Me.") In his autobiography, Miles admired his "concept of space, his lightness of touch, his understatement, and the way he phrase(s) notes and chords and passages." Clearly, Ahmad Jamal is a living legend.

He was born in Pittsburgh, Pennsylvania on July 2, 1930, and began playing the piano at the age of three. His teachers included Mary Caldwell Dawson and James Miller. His earliest influences were Art Tatum, Teddy Wilson and Erroll Garner. At the age of eighteen, he played his first professional job with the George Hudson Orchestra, which toured all over the United States.